Anabelle Takes a Hike

By Mitzi Cherry Moye
Illustrations by Lauren Adair Jones
Edited by Melissa Howard Lambert

ISBN: 978-0-9864490-0-0 Cherry Publishing

DEDICATION

This book is in honor of the many brave women I have known- my mother, Lena Davis Cherry who lived a long life filled with heroic deeds, daughter Holly who bravely fights for lives every day, and daughter Brittany who shares in that battle.

Melissa's editing expertise and Lauren's creativity made this book possible.

There is a huge cast of supporting characters in this league of women – Pam, Mattie, Beth C, Gibbs, and Mama Jo, Georgia and Elizabeth, Ann W, Beth M and Lisa T, Cindy, Lisa B, Michelle, Vicki, Karen, Leslie and Melissa, and most dearly - my brave and beloved fellow hikers: Carolyn, Nina, Jaclynn and Winston.

You mean the world to me.

ACKNOWLEDGMENTS

Everyone knows it – he's the love of my life... To Andy

To my grandchildren, great nieces and nephews -
May you be brave, appreciate art, and enjoy this beautiful world

Anabelle is a brave girl.

Sometimes
she feels
a little
scared of
something,
like a creepy
bug, or
a dark
shadow, or a
loud noise.

But mostly, she is brave.

She does brave things,

like taste broccoli,

or surf a wave,

or meet a new friend.

Sometimes Anabelle helps others who aren't so brave. She helped Lila take her first bite of watermelon.

Anabelle likes watermelon.

Lila didn't like it.

Anabelle helps
Lawson enjoy
the beach.
The first time
he jumped a
wave, he was a
little bit scared.

But by the fourth time, he loved it.

Anabelle tries to play golf with her bigger cousin Will.

She isn't very good, but at least she tries.

Anabelle doesn't like everything she tries.
She doesn't like high heels or pink
medicine. She doesn't like sitting still
and listening for a long, long time.

But she keeps trying. As she tries
more things, her bravery grows.

There are woods near Anabelle's house, with a trail going into the trees. One day, she was feeling especially brave, and decided to go for a hike.

The trees were huge and the path was rocky, but she wanted to explore this new place.

Anabelle wanted to try.

It looked a little scary.

She invited her cousins to come along because...

sometimes things are a little less scary if you have your family or friends with you.

They were all a little scared, but
Anabelle promised to lead them
(and they asked Grandma to come along).

Together, they planned for what they would
need on the hike. They packed water and
snacks in their
backpacks and made
sure that their shoes
were tied tight.

Lawson was the youngest and did not

know how to tie his shoes.

Charlotte helped him.

Off they went into the woods. The trees were so tall. They had to step over big roots and pay attention to the trail.

It was an adventure!

While they walked they sang songs and laughed. Their legs were tired, but being together made it fun. Anabelle was not even afraid of the bugs. She felt safe with her cousins.

They reached a clearing in the woods and discovered a pond. "I never knew this was here," said Anabelle. The cousins cheered, "We found a special place!"

They sat beside the pond and shared snacks. All around them were new things – birds singing, frogs croaking and even a fish jumping out of the water.

It wasn't scary at all!

"We need to be sure that we are back before dark," said Anabelle.

Before they left, they cleaned up from their snack, and each found one smooth rock to take as a reminder of the hiking adventure.

As the cousins grew up, their rocks reminded them of their bravery.

Sara put her rock in her backpack for her first day of school.

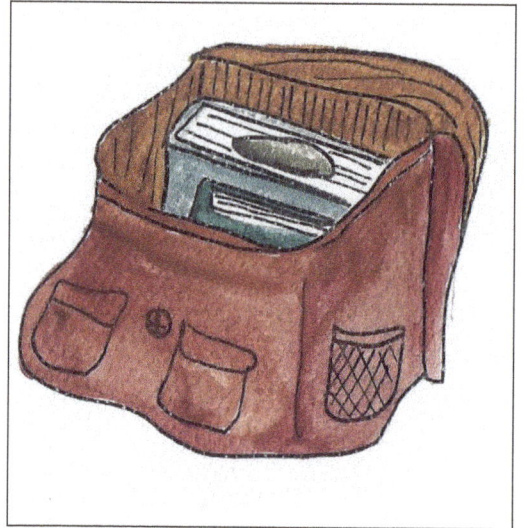

Davis put his rock in his pocket when he made his first trip to the dentist.

Lawson collected more and more rocks.

He loved exploring new places.

For every new adventure, the rocks reminded each of them of a time when something was a bit scary, but they were brave.

Almost every day, they tried something new. They were glad that Anabelle was brave and hiked with them. And as they slept each night, they dreamed of the exciting adventures ahead.

THE SPIDER AND THE VEGETABLES

Dennis P. O'Neill

Illustrations by Blueberry Illustrations

THIS BOOK BELONGS TO

_____

To My Mom and Dad, My Grandparents,
and All Of The Other Story Tellers
From My Old Irish Roots

May all of these stories live on in the hearts
and minds of Those who read them. May
they apply the wisdom that they read
About in them to their young lives

Once upon a time there was
a very poor family that lived
in a small farmhouse in western
Pennsylvania. The mother and
father had two small children….
a young girl named Laura and
her younger brother named
Brian who was just five years
old at the time of this story.

Now their father was named John.
He had to take a job in a nearby
brick factory to earn enough money
to pay off some of their many bills.
He worked long hours every day
and he often came home so tired
that he didn't even feel like eating
any supper. He hardly ever had
any time or energy to play with his
children, but when he did, Laura
and Brian had a wonderful time.

Carol, their mother, worked hard
out in the fields of their small farm
every day. She plowed the fields with
her tractor and planted many rows
of vegetables and berries. Later that
summer she was hoping to sell
her crops at her small farm stand
down by the road. Every morning
she would get up real early to
make breakfast for everyone
and to prepare nice lunches
for her children and husband
to enjoy later in the day.

During the day it was Laura's
job to babysit her younger
brother. At lunchtime every day,
she would heat up her mother's
specially prepared lunches for
them to enjoy. This day she
heated up on the stove some
vegetables and ham for them to eat.
"Now make sure you eat all of
your vegetables or you won't
grow up to be a strong boy!"
Laura said to her little brother Brian.

Brian looked over at his older
sister's face and frowned. Every
day she ordered him to eat all of his
vegetables and he hated eating them.
Laura quickly ate all of her lunch
and then took her empty dish over
to the sink to wash it out. Brian
watched her very carefully for a
chance to empty his vegetables out
the open kitchen window behind
him. When he was sure that she
wasn't watching, he quickly dumped
his plate of carrots out the open window.
Brian smiled to himself at how easily he
had been able to trick his older sister.
He thought to himself that if he was
very careful, he could fool his sister
and mother into thinking that he was
eating all of his vegetables every day.

About a month later, Brian and Laura were sitting at the kitchen table eating their lunches together. Laura once again finished eating her lunch first and so she got up to wash her dish in the sink. Brian rose up from his chair and quickly poured his remaining vegetables out the open window. This time, however, he forgot to take his fork out of his plate and so it was also poured out the open window. His face became beet red in fear that his sister would discover what he had been doing all summer long with his vegetables. He had to get his fork outside and quickly. "I'm all done Laura…I'm going outside to play!" he shouted as He ran out the back door.

Brian ran down the rear steps and over to the open kitchen window. He expected to see a big pile of vegetables on the ground next to his fork, but he only saw his uneaten broccoli. He guessed that the insects and small animals had eaten all of his previous plates of cooked vegetables.

As he reached down to pick up his fork on the ground, his eyes caught sight of a big hairy spider looking over at him from under the porch roof. Brian felt very scared. He wanted to run away, but his small right foot was stuck on a thin web that led over to the porch and spider. Brian struggled to pull his right foot free from the web, but it held onto his sneaker tightly.

"Laura! Laura, help me! A huge spider has caught me in his web and is trying to eat me!" he shouted up towards the open kitchen window.

Brian watched in horror as the
spider began to pull on the web.
He fell down on the ground and
tried to crawl away from the spider,
but the web was very strong and
held him there. Suddenly, he felt his
big sister's strong arms around his
shoulders. She pulled on him, but
the web was very strong. She
tried to pull on him once again
with all of her strength and the
web snapped. He was free.

The two of them ran away from the
porch area together. When they got to
the side of the house, Laura yelled at him.
"How could you have been so wasteful?
I saw your fork on the ground next to the small
pile of broccoli. Because of your foolishness,
you got caught by that big spider! If I hadn't
come out of the house when I did, he might've
been able to pull you into his web! That
spider only got as big as he did because
he was eating all of your vegetables."
"I'm sorry Laura; I'll never waste any
of my vegetables ever again. I want to
grow up even bigger and stronger than
that mean old spider!" he said to her.

From that day forward, Brian ate
all his vegetables and everything else
that his mother made for him to eat. Every
day he grew bigger and stronger. The spider,
however, got smaller and smaller and
soon disappeared from the porch area.

THE END

Dennis P. O'Neill is a published author
whose love for writing has been shown in his two
previously published novels. *Mortal Images
and The Sparkman Incident.* His unique gift
for writing and telling stories to children
finds its roots in his deep Irish heritage.
His childhood memories were filled with
many wonderful stories from his parents and
grandparents. His many fiction and nonfiction
stories, as well as his many wonderful illustrations,
will both captivate and entertain the minds
and imaginations of his many young readers.

www.ingramcontent.com/pod-product-compliance
Lightning Source LLC
Chambersburg PA
CBHW040257100426
42811CB00011B/1296